Clip-Art Sentence Sermons 2

Clip-Art Sentence Sermons
for Church Publications 2

George W. Knight, Compiler
Howard Paris, Illustrator

BAKER BOOK HOUSE
Grand Rapids, Michigan 49516

Copyright 1988 by
Baker Book House Company

ISBN: 0-8010-5495-8

Third printing, May 1990

Printed in the United States of America

Local congregations may clip and publish these sentence sermons in publications circulated among their church church members without securing permission. Publication in denominational and general religious periodicals without permission is prohibited.

Contents

Sermons to Make You Smile   7

Subject, **number**, page

Action, **1–6**, 11
Advice, **7**, 13
Age, **8**, 13
Behavior, **9–11**, 15
Blame, **12–13**, 15
Blessings, **14**, 17
Children, **15**, 17
Christmas, **16**, 17
Computers, **17**, 19
Criticism, **18–20**, 19
Duty, **21**, 21
Expectations, **22–23**, 21
Flattery, **24–25**, 21
Future, **26**, 23
Giving, **27**, 23
Goals, **28–30**, 23
God, **31**, 25
Happiness, **32**, 25
Ignorance, **33**, 27
Impatience, **34**, 27
Intelligence, **35**, 27
Interpersonal Relationships, **36–40**, 27
Leadership, **41**, 31
Mistakes, **42–45**, 31
Modesty, **46–48**, 33
Money, **49–51**, 35

Nosiness, **52**, 35
Opportunities, **53**, 37
Past, **54**, 37
People, **55–56**, 37
Planning, **57**, 39
Prayer, **58**, 39
Prejudice, **59**, 39
Pride, **60**, 39
Progress, **61–62**, 41
Prosperity, **63**, 41
Self-concept, **64**, 41
Self-pity, **65**, 43
Selfishness, **66**, 43
Service, **67–69**, 43
Sin, **70–71**, 45
Smile, **72**, 45
Success, **73**, 47
Tact, **74–76**, 47
Talk, **77–87**, 49
Temptation, **88–89**, 53
Trouble, **90**, 55
Truth, **91–92**, 55
War, **93**, 57
Wisdom, **94–95**, 57
Words, **96–97**, 57
Work, **98–100**, 59
Worry, **101–03**, 61

Clip-Art Sentence Sermons 2

Sermons to
Make You Smile

Churches of all denominations responded enthusiastically to the first volume of *Clip-Art Sentence Sermons for Church Publications,* released by Baker Book House in 1986. So here's another compilation of these illustrated humorous sayings. They are guaranteed to put a little lighthearted fun into your publications while communicating a spiritual message at the same time. Church members love sentence sermons because they are interesting and funny and they deliver their message in an instant.

If you need a sentence sermon on a specific subject, refer to the contents page at the front of the book. Here you will find the sentence sermons identified by number and keyed to a handy subject index that helps you find exactly the one you are looking for.

All these sentence sermons are copyright-free to local churches. Just clip them out of the book and paste them down on your newsletter or publication layout sheet for quick-and-easy reproduction by copy machine, electronic stencil, or offset press.

Our thanks to all who made our first compilation of sentence sermons a success. We hope these prove to be just as practical and popular in church publications.

George W. Knight
Howard Paris

How to Work a Plan

Almost any system will work if the people behind it do.

Life's Greatest Mistake

The only way to keep from making mistakes is to do nothing—and that's the greatest mistake of all.

The Personal Approach

"I must do something" will always solve more problems than "something must be done."

Ideas: Made to Work

Don't entertain ideas; put them to work.

The Power of Demonstration

Five minutes of demonstration are worth more than an hour of talk.

Better a Has-been

It's better to be a has-been than a never-was.

Wise People

We all admire the wisdom of those people who come to us for advice.

Don't Wait Until 40

It's true that life begins at 40, but you will miss a lot if you wait that long.

Criticized for the Right

It is better to be criticized for doing right than praised for doing wrong.

Lighting the Way

Always carry your own light, and you will never be in the dark.

Universal Life Principle

It's later than we think, and most of us aren't thinking.

Desperation Move

We usually don't blame ourselves until we have exhausted all other possibilities.

A Sure Sign of a Failure

A person hasn't failed miserably until he begins to blame others for his failure.

Prescription for the Blues

When you are discouraged,
Don't sit down and frown;
Just get a piece of paper
And write your blessings down!

No Secrets!

The best way to find out about your neighbors is to talk to their children.

Where Christmas Swells

If you don't have Christmas in your heart, you won't find it under a tree.

Thoughtless Computers

These new computers do everything but think—which makes them almost human.

Constructive Results

If you must hammer, at least *build* something.

An Easy Job

Fault is the easiest thing in the world to find.

The Knock that Hurts

Hard knocks won't hurt you—unless you're the one doing the knocking.

Ourselves Excused

Duty is generally what we expect of other people.

Mercy, Not Justice

Most of us aren't satisfied when we get exactly what we deserve.

The Universal Desire

Most of us want the same thing out of life—more than we deserve.

The Lies Easy to Believe

It's hard not to believe a liar when she's saying nice things about you.

Slapping and Swallowing

The person who is slapping you on the back may be trying to get you to swallow everything he tells you.

The Uncertain Future

Don't let the future scare you; it's just as shaky as you are.

The Art of Receiving

The Lord loves a grateful receiver as well as a cheerful giver.

Face the Right Way

The direction we happen to be facing has a lot to do with our final destination.

Eyes Straight Ahead

Obstacles are those scary things we see when we take our eyes off our goals.

To Be Possessed

What a person possesses is not as important as what possesses him.

In God's Hands

Earthquakes and storms are God's way of reminding us that we don't have everything under control.

Success or Happiness

Success is getting what you want; happiness is wanting what you get.

33

Danger: Ignorance Leak!

Keeping your mouth shut certainly keeps a lot of ignorance from leaking out.

34

Impatience Defined

Impatience has been defined as "waiting in a hurry."

35

Deep-flowing Stream

Intelligence is like a river; the deeper it flows the less noise it makes.

36

Wall Builders

Most people are lonely because they build walls instead of bridges.

Rude People!

Some people have the nerve to go right on talking when you're interrupting.

How to Lose Ground

Remember that mud thrown is ground lost.

No Cause for Worry

We wouldn't worry so much about what others think of us if we knew how seldom they do.

No Good Accomplished

Being told for your own good seldom does you any.

No One to Follow

Good leaders are so scarce these days that many people are just following themselves.

Plowing New Ground

If you must make mistakes, try to make a different one every time.

How to Avoid Extra Work

Efficiency is the ability to avoid extra work by doing it right the first time.

Looking on the Positive

A mistake is clear evidence that at least somebody tried to do something.

Don't Stop to Explain

The person who takes time to explain his mistakes has little time left for anything else.

A Common Commodity

Everyone has something to be modest about.

Modesty Is . . .

Modesty is the art of encouraging others to find out for themselves how important you are.

How to Boast Quietly

Modesty is the art of boasting in a shy, retiring way.

Purpose of a Budget

A budget is an instrument that helps you live below your yearnings.

Keeping Up Appearances

Some people are always in debt because they keep spending what their friends think they make.

Considering the Alternative

In spite of the high cost of living, it's still a popular activity.

A Hard Thing to Do

One of the hard things about business is minding your own.

The Jumping Game

Ever wonder why we don't jump at opportunities as quickly as we jump to conclusions?

Put Yesterday Behind

Never let yesterday use up too much of today.

Not Written by Attorneys

Imagine the appeals, hedges, and objections if lawyers had written the Ten Commandments.

The World Goes On

How strange that the world does so well without the names that once made the headlines.

Advance Planning

Plan ahead. It wasn't raining when Noah built the ark.

Pray Harder!

When it seems hardest to pray, we should pray the hardest.

The Power of Prejudice

Prejudice is a loose idea, firmly held.

Pride's Peculiarities

Pride is a peculiar disease; it makes everyone sick but the person who has it.

Non-working Cranks

The wheels of progress are seldom turned by cranks.

Old and Experienced

Nobody knows the age of the human race. But we all agree it is old enough to know better.

No Need to Panic

One good thing about being poor is that you don't panic when the stock market falls.

Your Consent Essential

No person is strong enough to make you inferior without your consent.

Unproductive Sympathy

The only time sympathy is wasted is when you give it to yourself.

Super Small Business

The person who lives only for himself runs a very small business.

Indirect Light

Those who bring sunshine into the lives of others cannot keep it from themselves.

Good Works or Good Walk?

Jesus went about doing good. But most of us are satisfied with just going about.

Misplaced Emphasis

Some people spell service, "Serve us."

No Late Payments

The wages of sin are always paid on time.

The Devil's Art

The devil is an artist; he paints sin in very attractive colors.

Dressing Up the Truth

The naked truth is always easier to take when it comes dressed in a smile.

Success: A Realistic View

If at first you don't succeed—you're about average.

A Carefully Made Point

Tact is the art of making a point without making an enemy.

Thoughts Expressed

A tactless person is one who says what everyone else is thinking.

Tact Defined

Tact is the ability to shut your mouth before someone else wants to.

Often Opened by Mistake

Many things are opened by mistake—but none more often than the mouth.

Guard Your Lips

If your lips would keep from slips,
Five things observe with care—
Of whom you speak, to whom you speak,
And how and when and where.

How to Save Face

One sure way to save face is to keep the lower half tightly closed.

The Sounds of Nothing

The less some people know, the more anxious they are to tell you about it!

Don't Say It

There's nothing wrong with having nothing to say—unless you insist on saying it.

An Open-and-Shut Case

Why is it that the person with a closed mind always has an open mouth?

Mind Before Talk

It is much wiser to choose what you say than to say what you choose.

Flowing Water

Some people are like rivers—small at the head and big at the mouth.

Fearfully and Wonderfully Made

God gave us a mouth that closes and ears that don't—which should tell us something.

Talked into a Corner

A loose tongue often gets its owner into a tight place.

Too Much of a Subject

An authority is a person who can tell you more about a subject than you really want to know.

Constant Temptation

Opportunity knocks only once, but temptation is constantly at the door.

Resisting or Putting It Off?

Resisting temptation is more than just putting it off until nobody's looking.

Fruitful Trouble

One good thing about trouble is that it gives you something to talk about.

Unchanging Truth

People cannot change truth, but truth can change people.

Why Truth Hurts

Truth hurts. You would, too, if you were kicked around that much.

Man's Best and Worst

The tragedy of war is that it uses man's best to do man's worst.

True Wisdom

Wisdom is knowing when to speak your mind and when to mind your speech.

Dig Before You Leap

Digging for the facts is better than jumping to conclusions.

Sharp-edged Words

Blunt words generally have a sharp edge.

One Spoonful Will Do

Don't use a gallon of words to express a spoonful of thought.

Hard Work Essential

If you want a place in the sun, you have to expect some blisters.

A Love-Hate Relationship

A lot of people love their jobs; it's the work they can't stand.

Big Mistake

The biggest mistake an employee can make is to assume he is working for someone else.

Accumulating Worries

If another bad thing happens, it will be six months before I can worry about it!

Fruitless Venture

Worry never robs tomorrow of its sorrows; it only saps today of its strength.

Paying Ahead of Time

Worry is interest paid on trouble before it is actually due.